Franklin Roosevelt's Postage Stamp Quilt:
The Story of Estella Weaver Nukes' Presidential Gift

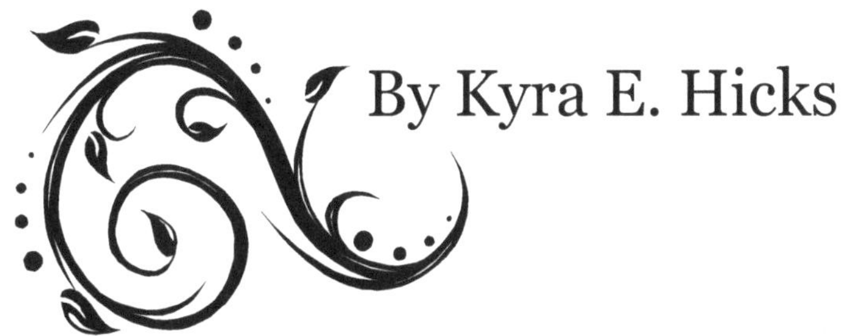

By Kyra E. Hicks

Black Threads Press
Arlington, Virginia

ISBN: 978-0-9824796-1-2

Library of Congress subject headings:

1. Nukes, Estella Weaver, 1888 – 1937 – Biography
2. African American quiltmaker – Indiana
3. Quilting – United States – History
4. Roosevelt, Franklin Delano, 1882-1945
5. United States – Works Projects Administration – Sewing Rooms

Cover Photo: Estella Weaver Nukes, courtesy of Hubert H. Nukes.
Cover Design: ManjariGraphics

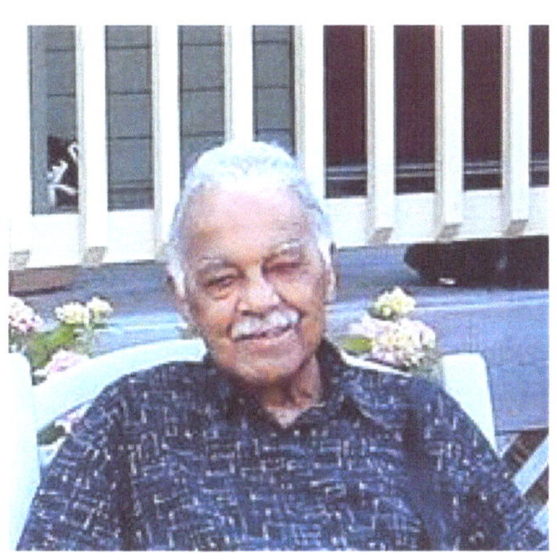

Hubert H. Nukes
November 6, 1927 - March 28, 2011

This quilt history adventure is dedicated to
the grandson who saw it all;
the generous man who shared it.

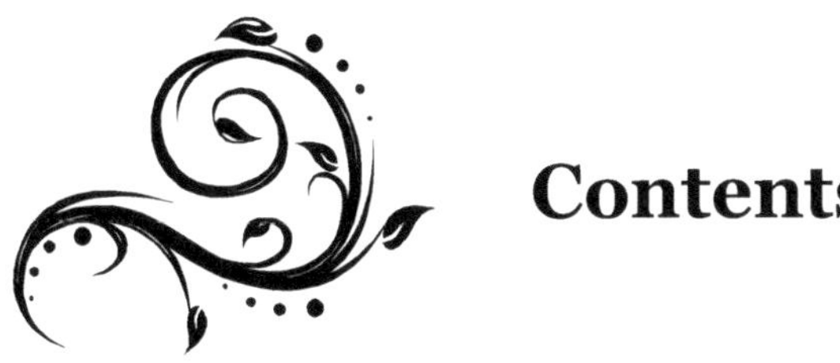

Contents

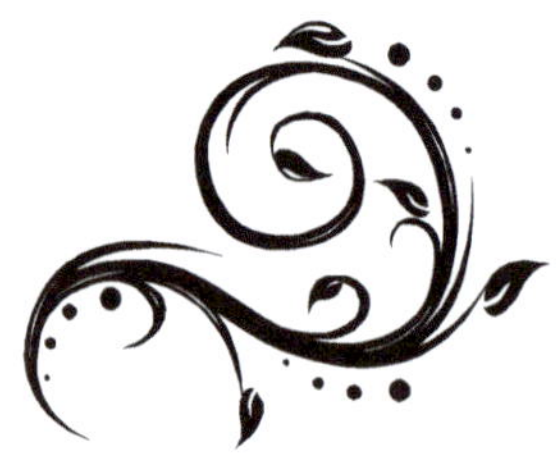

Acknowledgments

Quilt history research can be so adventurous, in part, because of the unexpected people one meets during the journey.

I'd like to thank Lynn Rude, the first person in the extended family of Estella Weaver Nukes that I met. I deeply appreciate her generosity in sharing family history, her introduction of other family members, and her continuous, enthusiastic support of the research.

I am also thankful to the late Hubert H. Nukes, Estella's grandson who shared stories of his grandmother and her quilt, and his wife of forty-eight years, Denise Nukes, who was equally open. I so appreciate the telephone interviews Mr. Nukes granted me.

During the research process, there were kind individuals at institutions who provided important insights and records. I'd like to publically thank Michelle M. Frauenberger, Collections Manager, Franklin D. Roosevelt Presidential Library; Katherine Hebert, Collections Manager, American Museum in Britain; Rutha M. Beamon, Archives Specialist at the National Archives; Dr. Sara B. Marcketti at Iowa State University; Dr. F. Kennon Moody, an extraordinary Roosevelt researcher; and Rhonda Stoffer and Betty A. Reynolds of the Marion Public Library.

Special appreciation is also given to Rosalind Webster Perry, granddaughter of Marion, Indiana quilter Marie Webster and Raleigh DeGeer Amyx and his wife, Hilda, for their time and historical insights.

Finally, I appreciate Grant County Historian William F. Munn for sharing Marion insights, articles, and for his personal introduction to individuals in Grant County.

I have diligently tried to ensure the accuracy of the historical narratives here and accept responsibility for any mistakes.

I hope you enjoy this latest quilt history adventure!

Kyra E. Hicks, f.w.c.
Arlington, VA

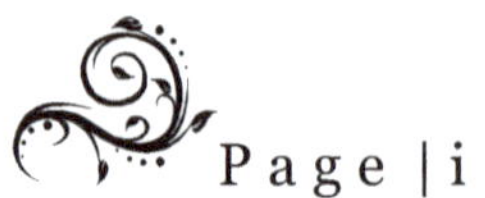

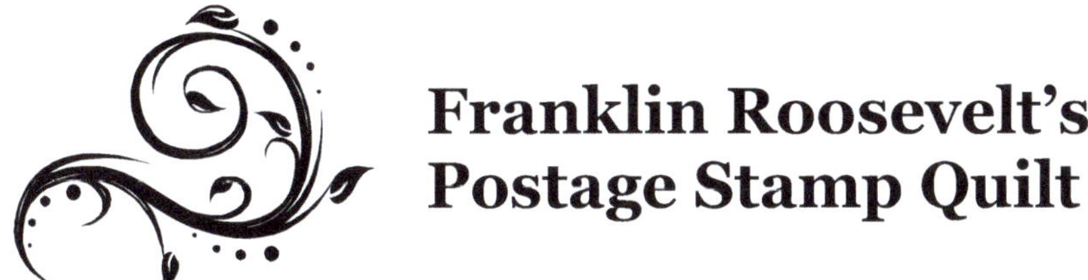

Franklin Roosevelt's Postage Stamp Quilt

I can think of only one, maybe two, activities more thrilling than an adventurous research visit to the Library of Congress. You have to understand: I have a collection of library cards from Kansas City to Ann Arbor, Los Angeles to London. But not even my cherished Readers Pass to the famed British Library compares to the esteem I have for my beloved Library of Congress Reader Identification Card.

What a privilege to have Library of Congress access to hundreds of delicious databases of articles or endless rolls of microfilm – each awaiting a discovery of some long-forgotten news story. With advances in electronic data storage and organization, the opportunity to make a discovery is seemingly just a keyword search away.

I "met" Estella Nukes on just such a Library of Congress visit.

While reading *War World II Quilts* by Sue Reich, I wanted to learn more about African American quilting contributions during this era. So, one Saturday morning, I ventured to the Library of Congress, stopping first for breakfast at Pete's Diner, a tiny, crowded and affordable eatery across the street from the library's James Madison Memorial Building, my final destination. Inside the Madison Building is the Newspaper and Current Periodicals Reading Room. Here I searched African American newspapers of the 1930s and 1940s for articles about quilters who made pieces during the Depression or in support of the war effort. During the 1930s, the Black press spanned the country in publications such as the *Atlanta Daily News*, the *Baltimore Afro-American*, the *Los Angeles Sentinel* and more.

Searching a database of African American newspapers, I typed a combination of keywords in search of articles: Negro, quilt, quilter, sewing, patchwork.

One resulting 1937 headline from the *Pittsburg Courier* read:

President Roosevelt Gets Present Of Novel Quilt Designed By Indiana Woman

"Marion, Ind., Jan. 7 (ANP) – A novel quilt, called the "postage stamp quilt," because its pieces are no larger than a postage stamp, and bearing the initials, "F.D.R." was pieced and designed by Mrs. Estella Nukes of this city, and later, after being exhibited in department store windows here, in Fort Wayne and Indianapolis, was sent to Washington, D.C., as a gift to the President of the United States.

"The quilting and embroidery work was done by members of the WPA Sewing class at the Marion civic hall, under supervision of Mrs. Ferol McMillian. Mrs. Nukes won wide commendation for the handiwork. She is the sister of Capt. Archie L. Weaver of Chicago, for twenty years executive secretary of the Chicago Branch N.A.A.C.P. and the recipient of a medal commemorating his long service with that organization."

The story of Mrs. Nukes' quilt also appeared on January 2, 1937 in the *Chicago Defender*. It said, in part:

Stamp Quilt Is Given to Mr., Mrs. Roosevelt: Indiana Woman's Gift Draws Attention

"Mrs. Estella M. Nukes of Marion, Indiana, presented to President and Mrs. Franklin D. Roosevelt, a so-called, "Postage Stamp quilt," which is creating wide comment in Indiana, Washington and other sections of the country . . .

"Upon completion of the unusual work of art, the work was placed on display in a Marion department store where it was viewed by thousands.

"Mrs. Nukes designed the entire product and hundreds of compliments have come to her from the beautiful handicraft. . .

"Besides Marion, the quilt was on display in Ft. Wayne, Indianapolis, and several other cities, and reached Washington in ample time to be displayed on the Roosevelt Christmas tree. A number of Marion women worked with Mrs. Nukes on the gift."

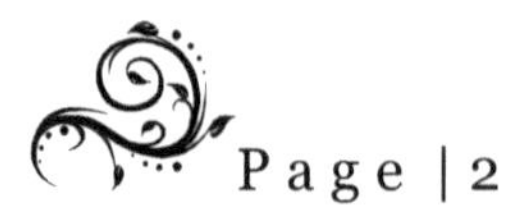

Who was this quilter, Mrs. Estella M. Nukes?

Estella May Weaver Nukes was born on January 28, 1888 in Grant County, Indiana. She came from a large family, with many step and half brothers and sisters. Her father, Franklin Weaver, was one of the early settlers in Liberty Township, Grant County, Indiana. Family history says he owned a coal yard. His last marriage was to Catharine Jones Burden, a widow and Estella's mother.

Newspaper accounts declared Catharine "of marvelous attractions." She was so lovely that one suitor murdered another man over her in 1874. Catharine married twice. Counting the children from her first marriage to William H. Burden and her union with Franklin, Catharine had nine off-springs: five boys and four girls. A few years after Franklin passed in 1892, Catharine Weaver had an affair with a minister at the local colored Baptist church and became with child. According to a newspaper account, the minister "was compelled to leave the city" after the affair became public knowledge. Sadly, both Catharine and her baby passed away in 1897, days after the baby's difficult birth.

Estella, then nine, and her siblings were sent to live with relatives.

Estella married Thomas J. Nukes on June 20, 1906. She was eighteen years old and he was thirty-three. The couple had seven children: four boys and three girls. One of the girls, Catherine Rebecca, had a son named Hubert Nukes.

In 2007, when I first "met" Estella Nukes at the Library of Congress, I set out to determine if Mrs. Nukes, who made the presidential quilt at least seventy-years prior, was still alive or if there were family members who could tell me about her and the quilt.

Through a request on a genealogy discussion board, I located a distant relative, who passed me along branches of the family tree, arriving at Mr. Hubert Nukes, grandson of Estella Nukes.

"I'm 83 years old!" Mr. Nukes said to me during one of our phone conversations. "I'm the oldest grandchild. I was born out of wedlock. She (Estella) and my grandfather reared me."

In his 70s, Hubert Nukes wrote a series of letters and reflections about his family that he shared with the family of Walter Archie Weaver, his uncle who passed away in 1997. Following is a short compilation of those writings about his grandparents, who he said affectionately were opposites in nature and personality.

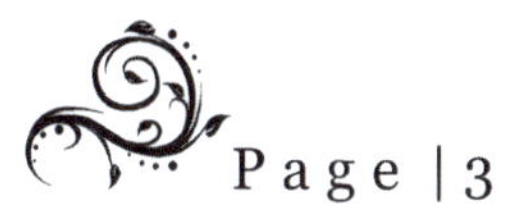

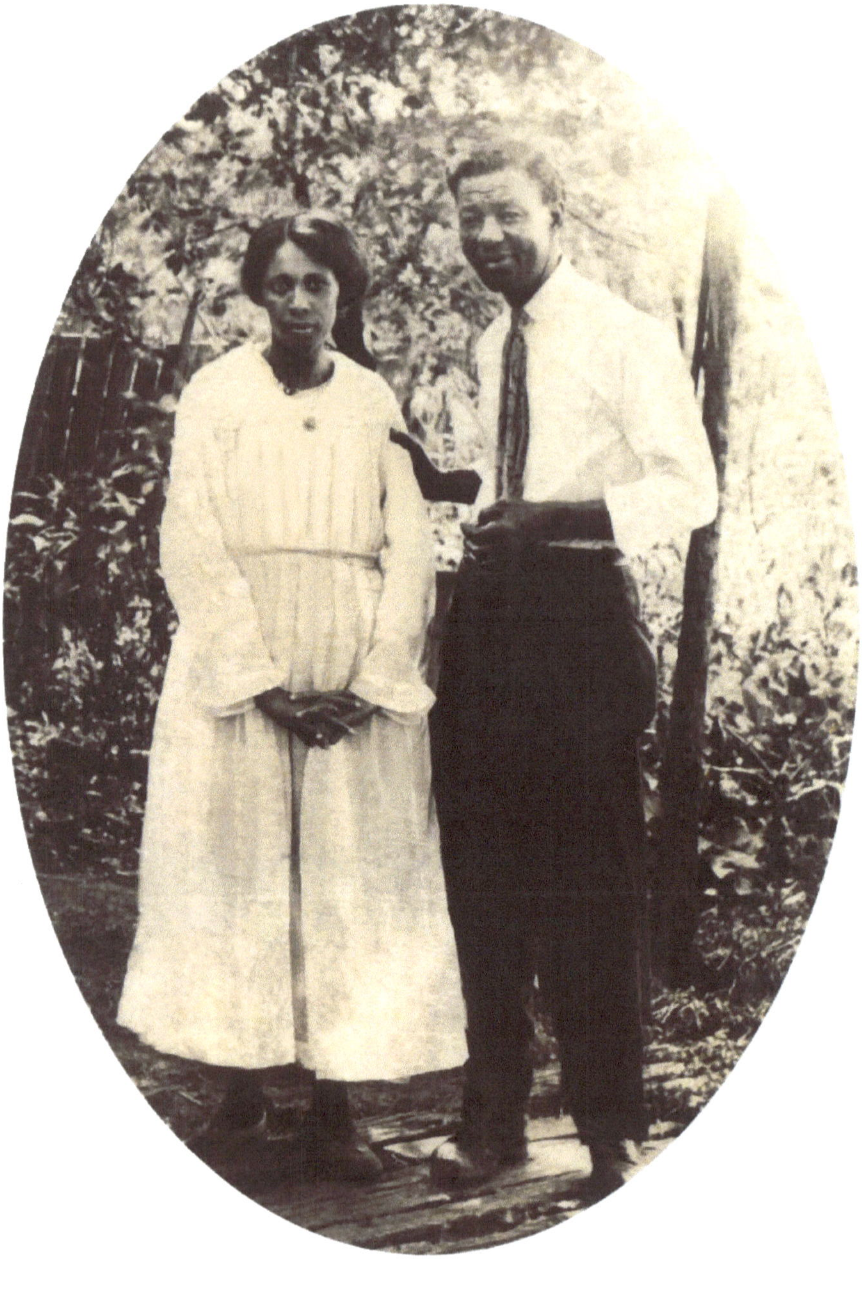

Estella Weaver Nukes and Thomas J. Nukes
Marion, Indiana, circa 1910 or 1917
Courtesy of Herbert H. Nukes

“Everyone knew Tom Nukes,” Hubert Nukes wrote. “He was the “foot doctor.” He also gave steambaths, a big thing during the depression, and massages. Tom had very high cheek bones, smoked Marvel and Chesterfield cigarettes and always had a smile . . . very gentlemanly. He was also a heavy drinker, but I don’t remember ever seeing him drunk! “Grandfathers,” as I called him, was seventy-six when he died. His hair was still straight and black and he had 30 teeth.

“Grandmother loved her family, her church, and her garden. Each spring, Monroe Harris, her cousin, would plan the lot on the alley. He had two big horses, Ned and Betty, for plowing. She planted everything and I helped: corn, tomatoes, cabbage, green beans, peppers, lettuce, you name it. She also had asparagus and strawberries. We had a large grape arbor about twenty feet long. Big purple grapes and bees. She canned everything and stored the potatoes under the house. She made jars of jelly to go with biscuits every Sunday morning. She loved her garden. Grandmother was also a “reader.” She recited poems and essays. She would always sing,” Mr. Nukes recalled.

“Each year,” he continued, “all of the cousins, sisters, aunts, uncles, etc. would come home. Grandmother was the secretary of the Jones-Shoecraft Reunions. These reunions, besides all the food, drinks, and games, were the audits: who died, who was born, who got married, who got divorced. All of her minutes and papers were destroyed in [a] fire.”

Estella Nukes was a Seventh-day Adventist and charter member of the Ephasus Adventist Church, No. 2.

Estella and Thomas lived at 1919 South Meridian Street in Marion, Indiana. “Unlike today, the doors at 1919 were never locked,” recalled Mr. Nukes. “There wasn’t anything to steal anyway.

“The house really needed painting. It also needed inside plumbing – especially in the winter. Walking fifty yards in seven inches of snow sometimes discouraged your need to go.

“The house had four rooms. There was a coal stove in the kitchen. In the summer the kitchen was really hot.

“We had a big stove in our living room. Baths were taken behind it in the winter. There was a pump-organ in that room. Grandfather and Aunt Elizabeth played on it. I remember them singing and playing.

“Our neighbors were German, Scotch, English and Irish. I remember all of the kids being at our house,” recalled Mr. Nukes.

Marion, Indiana in the 1930s was also the home of Marie Daugherty Webster (1859 – 1956), who in 1915 wrote, *Quilts: Their Story and How to Make Them*, the first book on American quilting. Her appliquéd quilts were published in the *Ladies Home Journal* in 1911 and 1912, leading many quilters nationally to request patterns for the quilts. Mrs. Webster opened a mail order pattern business and later founded the Practical Patchwork Company, a venture located in her home. Mrs. Webster lived in Marion at 926 South Washington Street until 1942, when she moved to Princeton, New Jersey to live with her son and his family. Today her house is designated a National Historic Landmark and is the home of the Quilters' Hall of Fame.

I wonder if Marie Webster knew or knew of Estella Nukes. Elizabeth Stewart, an African American resident of Marion born in November 1920, once worked for Marie Webster. She said of her teenage years in one oral history interview, "I had a job after school. I had to work for these people named Webster. And you would go there and you would help with the evening meal and you would ... do the dishes and clean everything up." Perhaps Elizabeth Stewart or the other help in the Webster household may have mentioned Mrs. Nukes' Postage Stamp Quilt to Marie Webster.

Both Elizabeth Stewart and Estella Nukes attended Allen Temple Church, though at different times, according to articles in the Black newspaper, the *Indianapolis Recorder*, and Mrs. Stewart's oral history interview. However, I haven't yet been able to confirm if the two families knew each other.

Hubert Nukes was not yet three years old when a profoundly tragic, scaring community event occurred in Marion, Indiana. One August 1930 evening, three jailed Black teenagers, Thomas Shipp, Abram Smith, and James Cameron, accused of murdering Claude Deeter and raping his date, Mary Bell, were forcibly taken from the jail by a mob. Shipp and Smith were lynched, an act hauntingly captured on film by Lawrence Beitler; even today, more than seventy years later, the photographs can be found through a Google search. James Cameron was rescued and later convicted of being an accessory before the fact to manslaughter. He served his term and probation. In 1982, Cameron self-published his life story, *A Time of Terror: A Survivor's Story*, founded the Black Holocaust Museum in 1988, was pardoned by the governor in 1991, and passed away in 2006. No one was ever convicted of the murders of Thomas Shipp or Abram Smith.

Might Estella Nukes have known the families of the lynched teens?

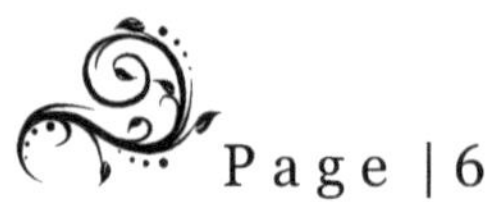

The Depression was still in force in 1935/36, when Mrs. Nukes is likely to have conceived the idea of making a quilt for President Franklin Roosevelt.

During President Roosevelt's first term in office, he sought to provide substantial relief from the Depression by creating new federal agencies that would employ civilians, among other goals. During his first 100 days in office, legislation creating agencies such as the Civilian Conservation Corps, the Public Works Administration, the Civil Works Administration and the National Recovery Administration, were formed. In 1935, the Social Security Act was passed and the Rural Electrification Administration and the National Youth Administration were instituted. The Works Progress Administration (WPA), later renamed the Works Projects Administration, was also created.

Several well-known programs were part of the Works Progress Administration, including the Federal Art Project, the Federal Music Project, the Federal Theater Project, and the Federal Writers' Project.

President Roosevelt ran for a second term in 1936, a most eventful year still remembered today. In January, England's King George V passed away. In March, construction of the Boulder Dam, later renamed the Hoover Dam after President Herbert Hoover, was completed. Margaret Mitchell's epic novel *Gone with the Wind* was published in May. Mary McLeod Bethune was named Director, Negro Affairs of the National Youth Administration, the first Black woman to head a federal office. The Summer Olympics in Berlin, Germany captured the world's attention through the medium of television. American Jesse Owens won four gold medals, including the 100-meter dash competition. By year's end, King Edward VIII, abdicated the throne for twice-divorced American Wallis Warfield Simpson, who he famously proclaimed as "the woman I love."

The Fourth of July 1936 was a festive time for the Nukes family, according to the *Indianapolis Recorder*. Estella and Thomas Nukes' son, Taylor Pierson married Miss Lorraine Vance at the parsonage of Allen Temple A.M.E. Church in Marion.

In 1936, Mrs. Nukes also participated in a WPA sewing project, according to her grandson and a *Pittsburg Courier* article.

A lesser known component of the Works Progress Administration was the WPA Sewing-Room Projects, which ran from November 1, 1935 to July 1, 1943. According to a scholarly article by Dr. Sara B. Marcketti, women accounted for 12% to 19% of all WPA workers. There

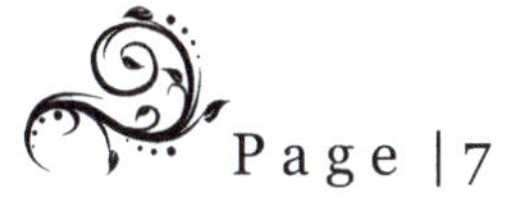

were 10,259 sewing rooms in operation by 1938. Though the exact activities were determined at the local level, in general, sewing room projects:

"... included places for the rehabilitation of old garments, dressmaking, the creation of household and hospital supplies, millinery, spinning and knitting of yarn, quilting, rug making, mattress making and collection of used clothing for renovation. Goods produced in the sewing shops were labeled, 'Made by Works Progress Administration, not for resale' ..."

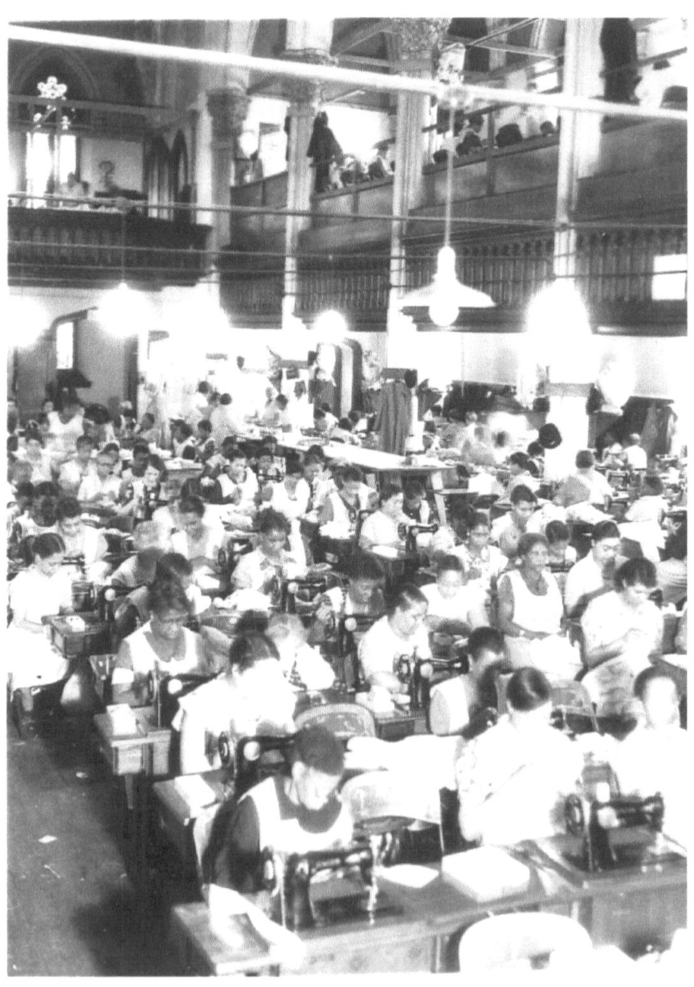

Washington D.C. Sewing Room, April 1938
The National Archives, 69-N-64

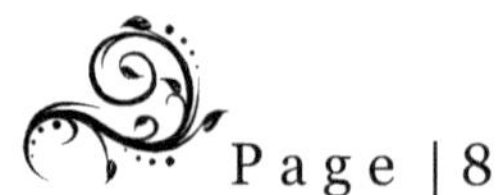

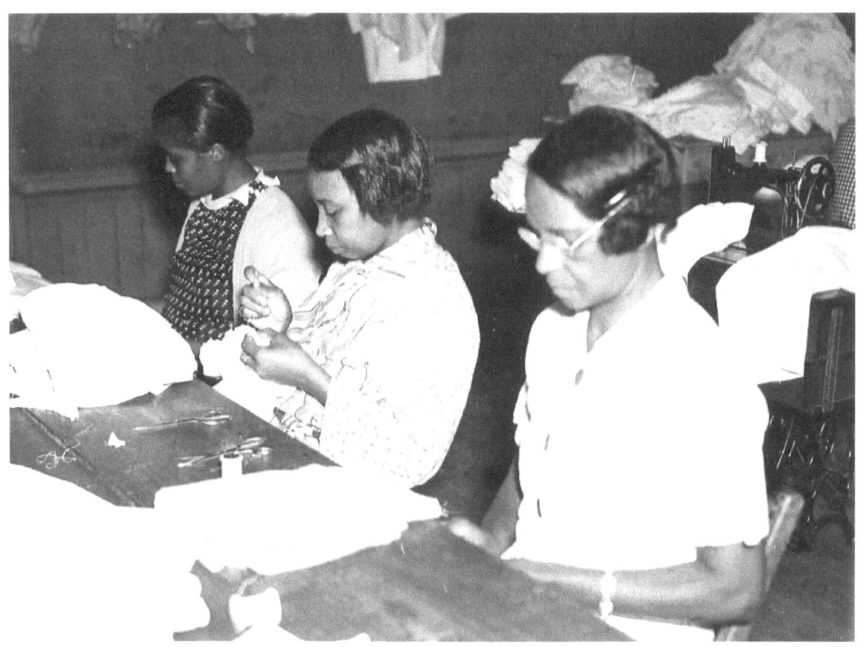

Negro Sewing Room, Harrisburg, PA, September 1936
The National Archives, 69-N-4334

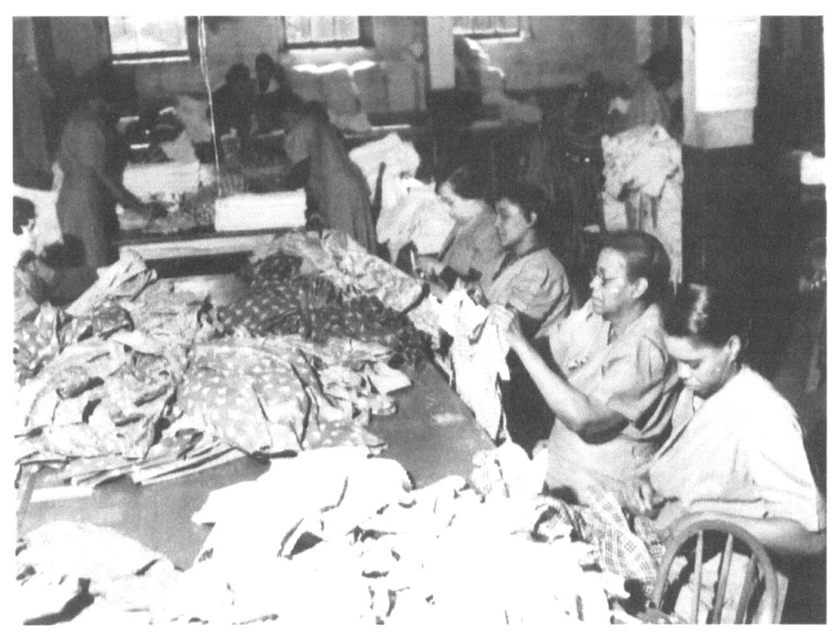

WPA Sewing Room, Chicago, IL, June 1940
The National Archives, 69-N-23547

According to the Associated Negro Press news agency, quilting and embroidery done on the Postage Stamp Quilt given to President Roosevelt "was done by members of the WPA Sewing class at the Marion civic hall, under supervision of Mrs. Ferol McMillan. Mrs. Nukes won wide commendation for the handiwork."

Hubert Nukes remembers that his grandmother, Estella Nukes, did not quilt professionally. However, she spent a year or two on this quilt.

"She was one of the original. There were ten or twelve other women involved overall. She was the initial one and the steady one," he said.

"Mrs. McMillan helped on the quilt, too," confirmed Mr. Nukes. "She lived about two blocks over. She was white. She had an apple tree. She had a habit of whipping me when I got in trouble. From 15th Street to 22nd Street, we [kids] would get a whipping if we were wrong!"

Ferol McMillan (1893-1949), a long-time Marion resident, was born in Markle, Indiana. She was prominent in the county Democrat Party. She attended Gethsemane Episcopal Church in Marion, "where she was soloist and had charge of the choir." According to her obituary in the *Marion Leader-Tribune*, Mrs. McMillan "was supervisor of the WPA sewing project here for several years when the federal aid program was in operation."

The Postage Stamp Quilt for President Roosevelt was exhibited in department stores in Marion, Fort Wayne and Indianapolis, according to the Associated Negro Press.

Hubert Nukes shared in one of our phone conversations that he remembered the newspaper men who came to interview his grandmother. He also remembered that the quilt was "regular bed size" and thought the quilt hung at the Hills Department Store in Marion, Indiana as well as displayed at City Hall or the Courthouse.

Quilting has been a necessary and social activity in Grant County, Indiana for some African American women. Mrs. Asenath Peters Artis, in writing about the Black community in Grant County during its first one hundred years (1812-1912), said of early homes: "The beds were high and filled with straw or shucks and feather bed weighing many pounds. Beautiful quilts, the handwork of the housewife, were numerous. The whitewashed walls and well-scrubbed floors showed an air of comfort." She penned those observations in 1914.

Barbara J. Stevenson-Spurgon recorded oral histories of African American Grant County residences born in the early 1900s. Her goal was to capture what daily life was like in the community. During one of those sessions, Delores Betts recalled the Ten-Si-Foy Club, active at least from 1900 - 1935. She said:

"The Ten-Si-Foy Club was a woman's social group in the Weaver (just outside of Marion) community. This is just women who happened to live in the community. Most of them had children who went to school... Anyway, they were a group of ladies who got together and quilted, and this was a necessary thing. It was fun to do, certainly, and the comradeship among them and exchange of news and discussion of problems and anything else that came along. It was a very productive think-tank, as well, and people – women – developed their own style of quilting, certainly, and that shows up in the designs that they did, but they would get together and make quilts or comforters or bring their sewing, you know, that needed to be done."

It is unclear if the making of the Postage Stamp Quilt by Estella Nukes and the other women of the WPA sewing group was inspired by the enthusiasm surrounding Franklin Roosevelt's 1936 Presidential campaign, which he overwhelmingly won.

During the 2008 U.S. Presidential Election, artists sought to capture the fervor and optimism expressed through the candidacy of then-Senator Barack Obama's campaign. Quilters were also very involved and literally hundreds of quilts, quilted wall hangings, and even quilted postcards were stitched. At least two exhibits of such art were organized. Susan Walen of Bethesda, Maryland curated *President Obama: A Celebration in Art Quilts* featuring works by sixty "ObamaQuilters" from across the country including Jeanette Thompson of Chicago, Carol Beck of Durham, NC, Deb Lacativa of Lawrenceville, GA, and Sabrina Zarco of Little Rock, AR. Dr. Carolyn L. Mazloomi curated *Journey of Hope: Quilts Inspired by President Barack Obama*, showcasing more than 100 quilts by quiltmakers including Renee Allen, Bisa Butler, Donnette Cooper, Carolyn Crump, Sylvia Hernandez, Peg Keeney, Penny Sisto, Jim Smoote and others.

The sheer volume of Barack Obama-themed quilts inspired quilter and folklorist Patricia A. Turner to develop a classification schema for such quilts. As she described in a 2009 American Studies Association

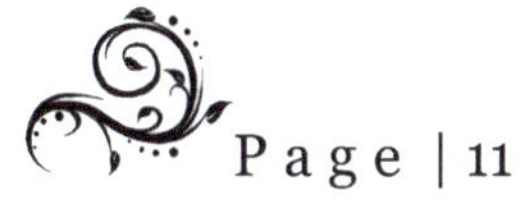

lecture titled "I Couldn't *Not* Quilt Obama," the four broad categories of quilts include:

1. **Portrait Quilts**: This category consists of Headshot Quilts with President Obama as the sole visual reference and Headshot Quilts with the president as the dominant, but not only visual reference.

2. **Pantheon Quilts**: Quilts where President Obama is included with others of significance to the quilter, though Obama is not necessarily the dominant image. Examples of such quilts have President Obama with other civil rights leaders, his family, other heroes and heroines, or the quilter or the quilter's family.

3. **Proxy Quilts**: Quilts featuring proxy icons for President Obama and the 2008 campaign, such as the use of the word "hope" in the font and colors used by the campaign or the red, white and blue flag inspired circle or logo of the campaign.

4. **Evocative Quilts**: This category includes quilts where the connection to President Obama requires an explanation by the quilter because a typical viewer of the quilt may not recognize the quilt as having an Obama theme or inspiration.

The quilt Estella Nukes designed, however, was not described as a portrait or narrative quilt. It was described as a Postage Stamp Quilt, with pieces the size of a first-class stamp! Barbara Brackman's *Encyclopedia of Pieced Quilt Patterns* places the postage stamp quilt in the category of quilt blocks composed of squares of equal size. The *Encyclopedia* lists thirty variations of one patch – square quilts. The pattern names include: Postage Stamp, Beautiful Mosaic, Building Blocks, Checkerboard, Crossword Puzzle, Sunshine and Shadow, Triple Irish Chain, and Trip Around the World.

During Franklin Roosevelt's four terms in office, several quilts were stitched for the president and his wife, Eleanor. Some of the quilts commemorated legislation and programs created by the president, while other quilt patterns were designed in honor of the First Couple.

Many quilters are aware that the *Kansas City Star* newspaper published over 1,000 quilt patterns from 1928 to 1961. Interesting patterns during the Roosevelt administration included: the *Square Deal* pattern (24 August 1932), the *Franklin D. Roosevelt* pattern (31 January 1934), the *Postage Stamp Quilt* pattern (18 February 1942), and the *President Roosevelt* pattern (17 May 1944).

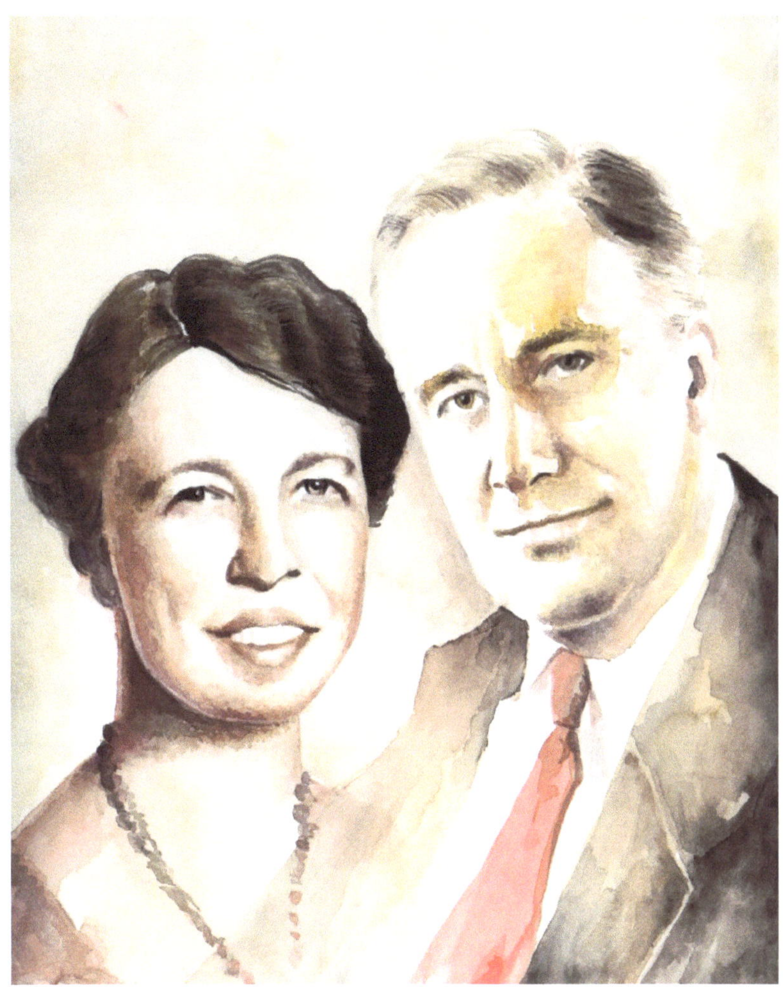

Eleanor and Franklin D. Roosevelt
Watercolor by Milan Ristic, 2012

National magazines and other newspapers also published quilt patterns in honor of the Roosevelts or articles about such quilts. In August 1933, *Needlecraft: The Home Arts Magazine* published the "Rose of the Field," an appliqued quilt featuring green leaves on white blocks. A row of flower buds along the top of the quilt symbolized the Roosevelt's five children. The quilt was designed in honor of President Roosevelt's first inauguration.

A December 30, 1933 *Montreal* (Canada) *Gazette* headline proclaimed "Quilt Given Mrs. Roosevelt." The story read "[a]ccepting an old-fashion quilt, the motif of which was "the Roosevelt Rose," the blossoms typifying the "new deal," Mrs. Franklin D. Roosevelt today expressed interest in a movement to stimulate among women with leisure the revival of quilt-making, as an all-American folk art."

In January 1934, the *Schenectady Gazette* published an article about Mrs. Ruth E. Finley designing the "Roosevelt Rose" quilt. The quilt, according to the article, "was presented to Mrs. Franklin D. Roosevelt by Miss Helen Koues, director of a national magazine fashion bureau."

Many publications reported news of the Roosevelt Rose quilt, including the *Chicago Daily Tribune* in an April 15, 1934 article by Needlework Editor, Nancy Cabot.

The White House continued to receive quilt gifts. In February 1935, Eleanor Roosevelt sent a note on White House stationary to Mrs. Jules Joseph Fischer of Mountain View, California, thanking her for the quilt she and other ladies gave to the First Lady, according to the note, now in the collection of Chicago quilter and history buff, Susan Wildermuth.

I can only imagine that Estella Weaver Nukes admired President Roosevelt and was grateful for the work, income, and camaraderie provided by the local WPA sewing project. But why did Mrs. Nukes select a Postage Stamp pattern to make a presidential quilt? Surely there were other more elegant designs? There is no documentation, yet found, to say definitively why this pattern was selected. It wasn't until I read more about the life of Franklin D. Roosevelt that I suspected I might have found a reason.

I believe Mrs. Nukes knew what others in the country did. President Roosevelt had a passion for stamp collecting!

Anthony P. Musso, a thirty-eight year Postal Service veteran and Brooklyn author of *FDR and the Post Office*, confirmed my suspicion in an email exchange:

"From my knowledge about FDR and the widespread attention that he brought to stamp collecting, I can totally understand why folks would make a quilt for him that featured postage stamps. FDR was very passionate about his collection and constantly spoke about it with great pride. The mindset of people around the world with regard to stamp collecting, which prior to FDR's years of public service was considered a child's hobby, changed when he became a public figure simply because of his keen interest and enthusiasm about it."

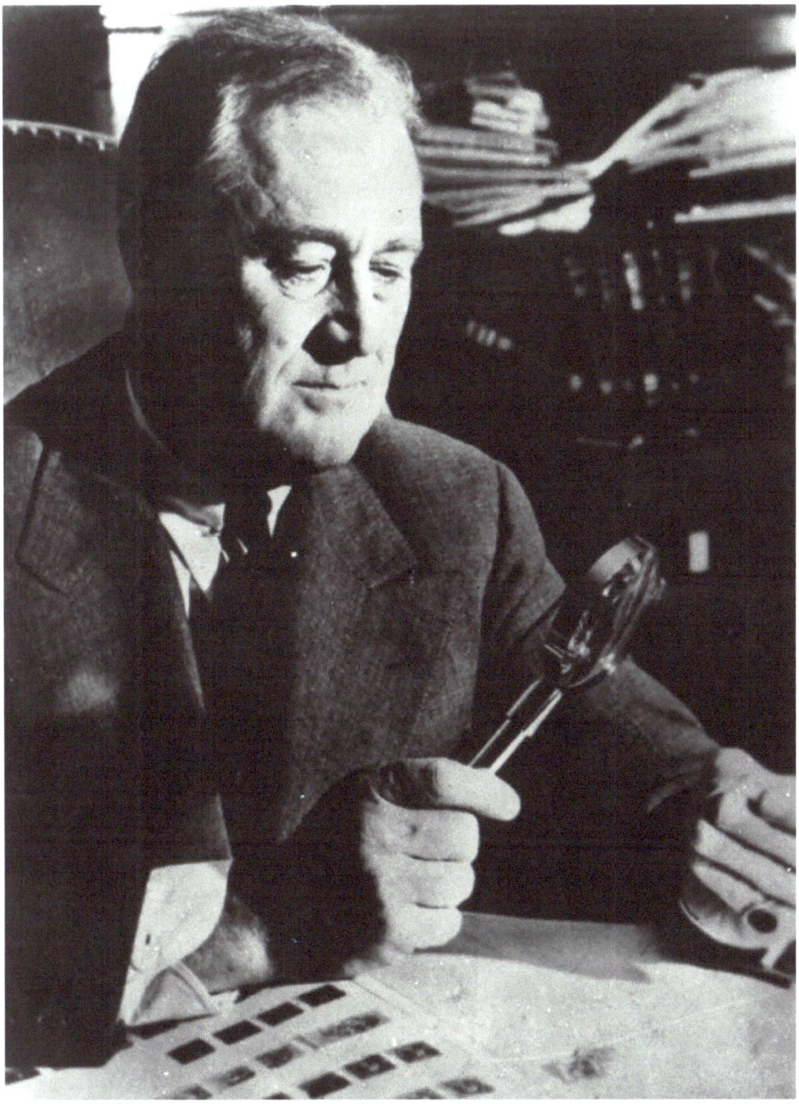

Franklin D. Roosevelt reviewing his stamp collection
Courtesy of the Franklin D. Roosevelt Presidential Library and Museum

Sara Delano, Roosevelt's mother, collected stamps as a young woman, including stamps from Hong Kong, where her family lived for a time. She passed her collection on to her younger brother, Frederic, who later gave the expanded collection to a young Franklin.

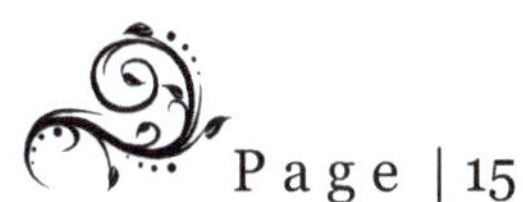

Franklin Roosevelt was said to have worked on the stamps daily, even while in the White House. Having such a prominent person as the President of the United States as a philatelist was a boon for the industry. According to author Brian C. Baur, at the start of the Roosevelt Administration in 1933, the president "had approximately 20,000 stamp specimens mounted in some 30 albums."

Lena Shawen, author of *A President's Hobby,* wrote that "[f]rom March 4, 1933, until his death on April 12, 1945, one hundred and thirty-four new commemorative and forty-nine new ordinary stamps were issued with his personal approval and supervision."

The president even designed selected stamps, including *In Honor of Mothers*, a 1934 Mother's Day first-class stamp.

From today's perspective, it is eye-opening to learn how popular stamp collecting was during Roosevelt's time in office. Newspapers across the country, including the *Washington Post*, employed stamp columnists. Starting in 1934, Proctor and Gamble advertised Ivory Soap nationally on the radio program *Ivory Stamp Club of the Air* featuring World War I Captain Tim Healy. Captain Tim used postage stamps as the inspiration for adventures around the world. Listeners, especially children, were encouraged to send 10¢ and two Ivory soap wrappers to the H. E. Harris & Co. of Boston for a Captain Tim 130-page stamp album or to send 4¢ and two wrappers to receive a packet of stamps to help fill the album. Don Schilling, host of *The Stamp Collecting Round-Up* blog, writes that "[b]y 1936, almost a million people had written in asking for the stamp album and over 2.5 million people had joined the stamp club. The show was responsible for distributing over 400 million stamps." The Captain Tim radio program ran from 1934 to 1945.

Quilt artist Dr. Carolyn L. Mazloomi collected stamps. She shared with me that "[a]s a young girl, in elementary school, I collected stamps and was quite passionate about the hobby. Ever since I can remember I have been interested in art and history. Each time I bought a packet of stamps was like opening a treasure...the brilliant colors, spectacular artwork, the history. Stamps represented historical events, people and places. As a child, I didn't have an opportunity to do a lot of traveling. My stamps allowed me to visit exotic places in my imagination."

When Roosevelt first ran for President in 1932, the American Philatelic Society issued a promotional stamp and envelope promoting one of its most famous members. Both items advertised "A Stamp Collector For President."

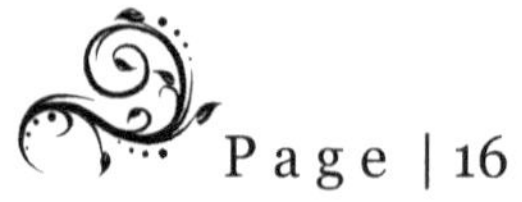

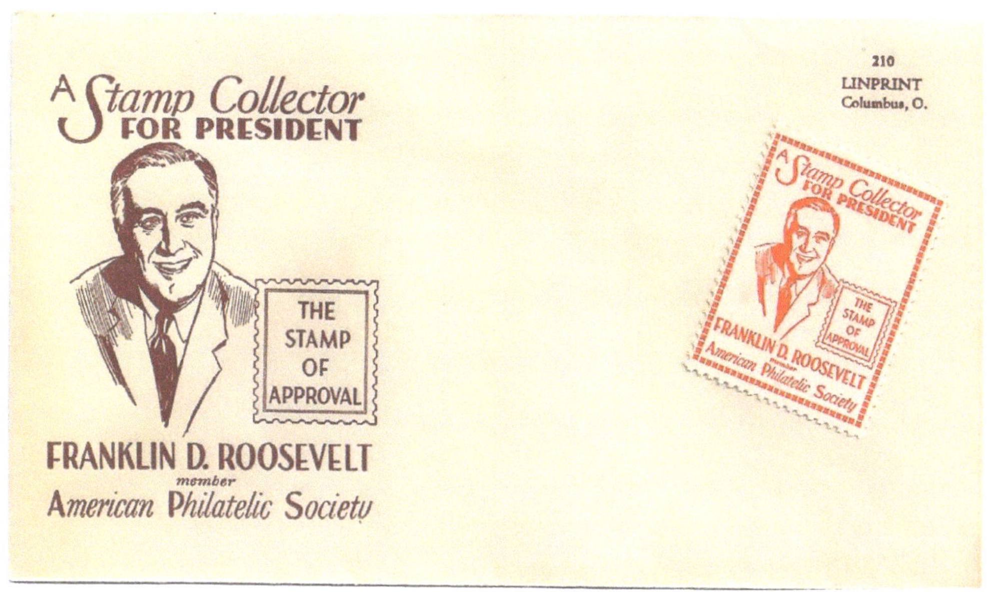

Envelope and stamp issued by the American Philatelic Society.

Yes, President Roosevelt greatly impacted stamp collecting. According to author Brian C. Baur, "[P]ost Office Department revenue was about $300,00 per year [in 1933]. At the time of the President's death in 1945, revenue had reached a high of $2 million per year."

Franklin Roosevelt passed away at his Warm Springs, Georgia cottage on April 12, 1945; witnesses said the President worked on his beloved stamp collection earlier that day.

The Postage Stamp Quilt stitched by Estella Weaver Nukes and other women in the WPA sewing project hung in a local Marion, Indiana department store before it was sent to be displayed in Ft. Wayne and Indianapolis, according to news reports. Then the quilt was sent to the White House in Washington, D.C.

How does one send a gift to the President of the United States? It's very simple. You can mail a gift to that famous address:

The White House
1600 Pennsylvania Avenue, NW
Washington, DC 20500

The Office of Presidential Correspondence includes the Gift Office, which documents and catalogs each gift sent to the First Family.

Bradley H. Patterson, a White House staffer in the Eisenhower, Nixon, and Ford administrations, outlined four potential outcomes for gifts sent to the First Family in his book, *To Serve The President: Continuity and Innovation in the White House Staff.*

All gifts, both foreign and domestic, as well as the gift's value and disposition, must be registered with the White House Gift Office. A determination is made on whether it is appropriate to keep the gift. Gifts deemed inappropriate are returned to the sender.

Gifts that are deemed acceptable, but that aren't kept by the First Family, are sent to the General Services Administration (GSA), to a charity or auctioned.

According to Mr. Patterson, gifts that are accepted by the First Family can be:

1. Deposited in a presidential library, given to the Smithsonian Institution, a cabinet department, or the National Zoo, for display;
2. Held in custody by the National Archives for possible future, personal retention of the First Family;
3. Added to the permanent collection of the Executive Residence, which is under the custody of the National Park Service; or
4. Kept for immediate personal use by the First Family. Gifts that are above certain "minimal value" must also be reported to the Office of Government Ethics. As of 2011, the Foreign Gifts and Decorations Act set the minimal value at $350, according to the GSA.

Presidents receive literally thousands of gifts during a single year. The William J. Clinton Library and Museum, according to its website, is the caretaker "for about 100,000 presidential gifts."

In President Roosevelt's administration, there wasn't such a formal, legal gift in-take and registry system. How might Mrs. Estella Weaver Nukes' Postage Stamp Quilt have been received by the White House in 1936?

Grace Tully, a secretary to President Roosevelt, wrote in her book about FDR that the Secret Service would x-ray packages arriving at the White House to ensure the contents were safe. Once deemed harmless, the package would be opened and sorted by a secretary in charge of gifts. Grace's sister, Paula Tully, held this position until 1940, then Mary Eben took over the Presidential gift responsibilities. Periodically, gifts would be sent to the president's Private Secretary to show the President. Tully shared that some gifts were given to staffers or sent to the president's personal home, library or the Oval Office.

As a child, Lillian Rogers Parks (1897-1997) occasionally accompanied her mother, Maggie Rogers (1874-1953), to work at the White House. Mrs. Rogers started working as a maid in the Taft Administration and retired as Head Housemaid in the Roosevelt era.

Mrs. Parks joined her mother as a White House employee at the start of the Hoover Administration, working as a maid and seamstress, even though she used a crutch after contracting polio in her childhood.

In 1961, Mrs. Parks fulfilled her mother's dream of writing a book about their White House experiences. With journalist Frances Spatz Leighton, she published *My Thirty Years Backstairs at the White House*. The biography spent twenty-six weeks on the *New York Times* Best Sellers List and later became a hit television miniseries starring Leslie Uggams as Mrs. Parks, Olivia Cole as Maggie Rogers, and Louis Gossett, Jr., Robert Hooks, Cloris Leachman, and Leslie Nielsen as various White House staffers.

In 1981, Mrs. Parks again joined Mrs. Leighton and published *The Roosevelts: A Family in Turmoil*. Here Mrs. Parks also confirmed that the president often gave gifts away. She wrote:

"FDR was not one to go shopping for presents for relatives or even to send anyone else out shopping. His generosity consisted of giving away the things that had come to him in droves – and he gave them all to his beloved grandchildren as well as to his offspring."

Mrs. Parks also wrote of the close, fond relationship she had with Missy LeHand, President Roosevelt's Private Secretary who lived at the White House in a "suite of rooms on the third floor, where [Mrs. Parks'] sewing room was."

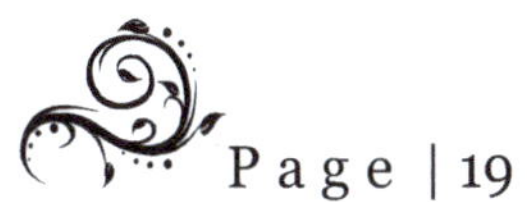

Missy LeHand, according to Mrs. Parks, "was somehow involved with everything FDR did for fun. Eleanor never showed any interest in FDR's stamp collection. Missy was an excited assistant collector, working on his collection with him and reminding him of where he had stashed some missing stamp."

I wonder if Missy LeHand ever invited Lillian Parks, the White House seamstress, to her office to admire any of the numerous textile or needlework gifts, including quilts, intended for the President and First Lady.

I also wonder if Mrs. Estella Nukes' Postage Stamp Quilt somehow received extra attention at the White House because the quilt was made of hundreds of little fabric pieces the size of President Roosevelt's own individual stamps. Did Paula Tully deliberately ensure Missy LeHand, and thus the President, saw Mrs. Nukes' hobby-inspired quilt? Or is it likely the President never saw the quilt given the sheer number of gifts that arrived constantly to the White House?

Where is Mrs. Nukes' Postage Stamp Quilt today?

Mrs. Parks served Franklin Roosevelt and the First Family for twelve years. Upon the death of the President, Eleanor Roosevelt invited Mrs. Parks and other close White House staffers into a bedroom where the First Lady had collected several personal, family items.

"Take what you want now," Eleanor Roosevelt said, according to Mrs. Parks, "because the rest is going to Hyde Park and you will never have another chance."

Mrs. Parks was given several items, including two bed covers which she described in two April 1983 letters:

"I was given this exquisite bedspread . . . owned by First Lady, Eleanor Roosevelt. It is one of the most beautiful pieces of handwork I have ever seen. I do not recall who may have given it to her. The double bedspread is handmade in the popular "Yo-Yo" quilt pattern for that day. It is made from pink, peach and white satin. It has two matching small pillows. It is so beautiful . . . It was in her White House Bedroom for a short time."

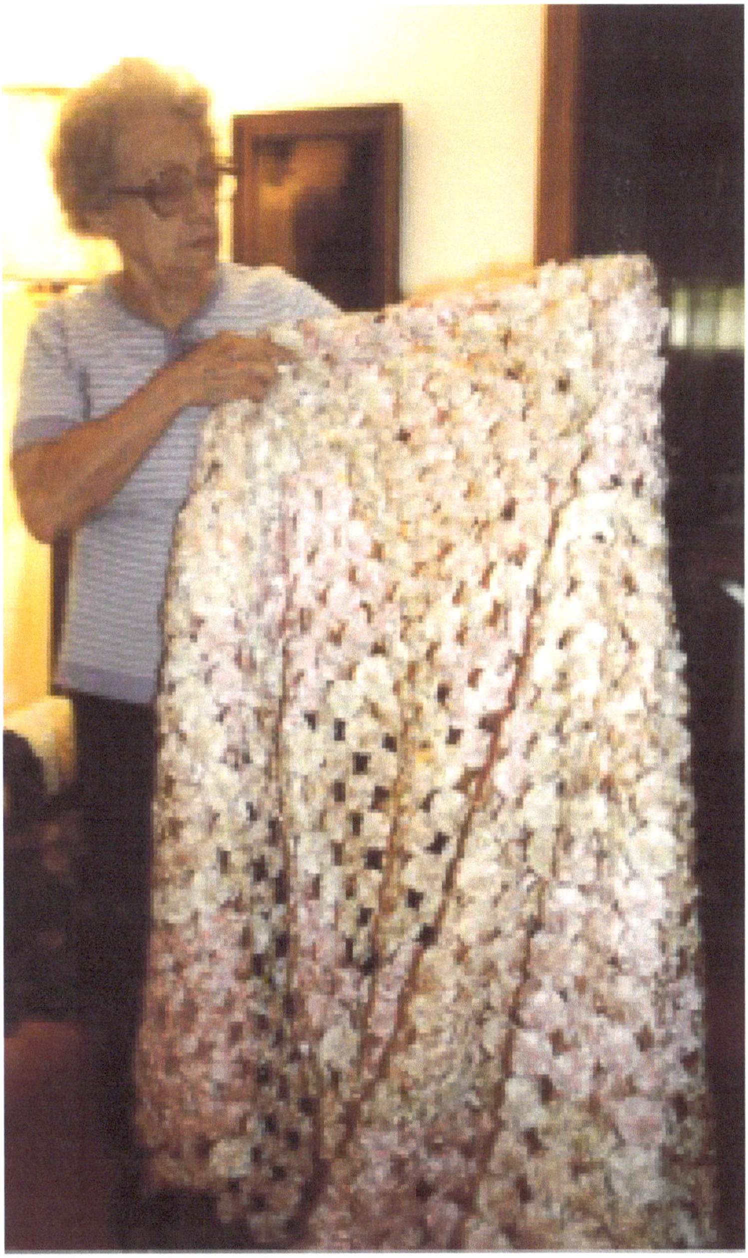

Lillian Rogers Parks holds a satin Yo-Yo Quilt, a gift
from Eleanor Roosevelt, who once owned the quilt, April 1983.
Courtesy of Raleigh DeGeer Amyx

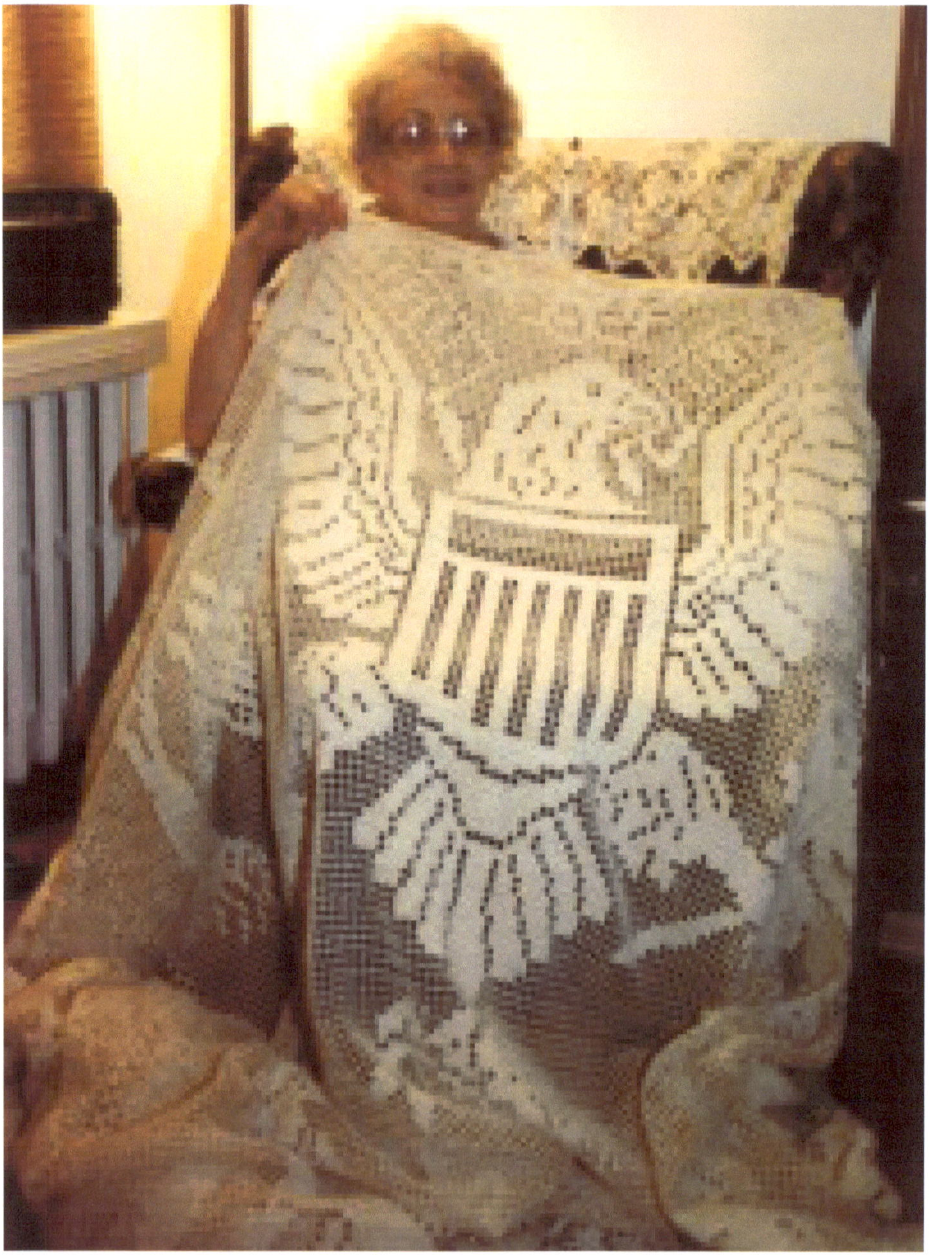

Lillian Rogers Parks displays a hand-crocheted Eagle Seal bedspread, which graced FDR's White House bed, April 1983.
Courtesy of Raleigh DeGeer Amyx

The second covering Mrs. Parks received held special significance.

"The bedspread was a personal possession of President Franklin D. Roosevelt," Mrs. Parks recalled. "The bedspread is expertly hand-crocheted. There is a large Seal in the top center. In the lower half below the Seal are two figures of Grecian-like Goddesses with children at their feet. Around the edges are peacocks which form a scalloped effect. It is a superior piece. . . It was on his White House bed at times. And, sometimes FDR's bedspread was used on the bed of important over-night diplomats, or his guests."

There is no record, as yet located, that Mrs. Parks ever saw or was given as a gift the Postage Stamp Quilt stitched by Mrs. Estella Nukes.

Would the Franklin D. Roosevelt Library and Museum in Hyde Park, New York have the Postage Stamp Quilt or a record of what may have happened to the quilt Mrs. Nukes and the ladies of the Marion, Indiana WPA Sewing project made?

There are nine quilts in the museum collection, according to Michelle Frauenberger, the registrar:

1. *Flower Quilt*, a pink and white silk quilt by Mrs. I. J. Freeman of Chicago, Illinois.
2. *Democratic Donkey Quilt*, showcasing the name of each U.S. state and the number of electoral votes FDR received in the 1936 election. Maker unknown.
3. *American Flag Quilt* by Mrs. Andy Hallford of Bangs, Texas.
4. *Shield of the United States Quilt* by an unknown quiltmaker. Presented to FDR by Willard H. Boyles of the Young People of the Church of God, Cleveland, Tennessee.
5. *Eleanor Roosevelt Portrait Quilt* by Callie Fanning Smith of Sulphur Springs, Texas, February 1940. Surprisingly, one of Mrs. Smith's pictorial quilts, similar in style to the Roosevelt quilt, is recorded in The Quilt Index website.
6. *NRA Quilt* was presented or sent to FDR by Jaske Bros. of San Antonio, Texas. According to research by quilt historian Sue Wildermuth, this National Recovery Administration quilt was stitched by Mrs. J. A. D. Robinson.
7. *Naval Quilt* by an unknown maker.
8. *NRA Crazy Quilt* by Petrina Peterson of Troy, New York, 1939.
9. *President Quilt* by Elizabeth Abele of Memphis, Tennessee, October 1943.

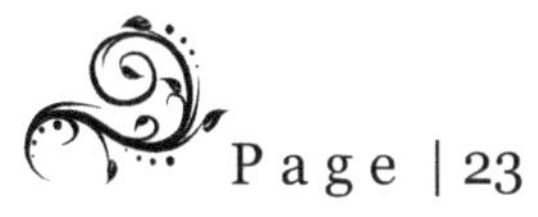

Ms. Frauenberger related that ". . . our Archival Department has searched its records for the gift of a quilt from Estella Nukes in 1936. Though a variety of sources were searched, no record of such a gift was found. However, what was found – and which may be of interest to you – was the mention in FDR's Gift File of a quilt sent to President Roosevelt from the Negro Home-making Class at Snow Hill, Seminole County, Florida. . . "

Surprisingly, Mrs. Nukes and the WPA Sewing Project in Marion, Indiana were not the only African Americans who wanted to show appreciation to President Roosevelt through a quilt gift.

In March 1936, R. L. Glenn, Chairman of the Seminole County Advisory Committee of the Florida Works Progress Administration sent a letter and quilt to President and Mrs. Roosevelt. He wrote:

> "This quilt was made by the Negro Home-making Class at Snow Hill, Seminole County, Florida, a project of the Education Department of W.P.A. Melissa Bacon of Snow Hill, Florida, is the teacher.
>
> "It is presented to you as a token of deep gratitude and appreciation for the timely help and the new hope which your practical social and economic program has brought to many of your people."

Missy LeHand, the Private Secretary to the president, sent a response to Robert L. Glenn, described by the 1930 Federal Census as an engineer. She wrote that the President and Mrs. Roosevelt "thank you for your courtesy in the presentation of that beautiful quilt, and have asked if [he] would not be good enough to convey to Mrs. Melissa Bacon and to the members of the Negro Home-making Class at Snow Hill, their cordial appreciation of the kind thought which prompted them to send this fine product of their work."

There is no detailed description of the quilt stitched by the Negro Home-making Class yet found. Sadly, this quilt is not in the Roosevelt Library and Museum's collection.

I suspect that Mrs. Estella Nukes' Postage Stamp Quilt was indeed received by the White House. The Secret Service would have x-rayed the package. Paula Tully, the gifts secretary, likely unfolded the covering and admired its craftsmanship. Why would I believe this?

There *was* a Postage Stamp Quilt gift in the Roosevelt family!

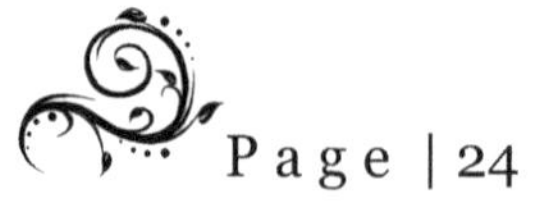

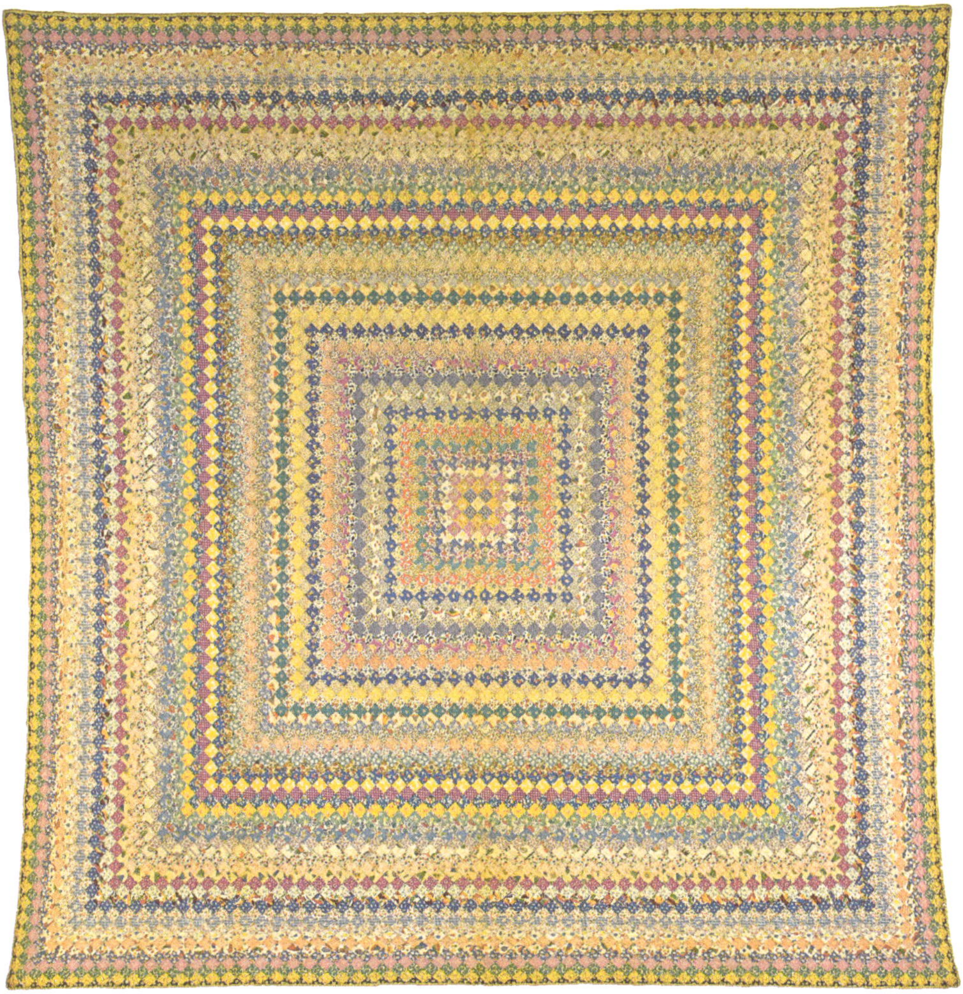

Trip Around the World Quilt, 1930s, 78" x 75"
Courtesy of The American Museum in Britain

Like Estella Nukes' grandson, Hubert Nukes, Curtis Roosevelt spent his childhood years living in his grandparent's "house" in Washington, DC. He and his older sister, Eleanor, were known by their nicknames "Sistie" and "Buzzie."

In 1941, Curtis' grandmother, First Lady Eleanor Roosevelt, gave a covering, called the Trip Around the World Quilt, to Curtis.

"My grandmother gave me a quilt that had been given to her, one made by a sewing group, I recollect, in 1939 or 1940," Curtis Roosevelt

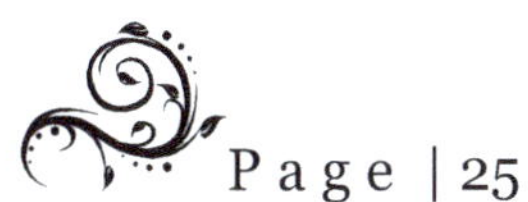

shared in an email exchange from France. “It was made with small squares, about an inch square. I used it for years, so it moved around the world. Finally, I had a choice of having it repaired or giving it to a museum. I gifted it to the American Museum in Bath for their collection of American quilts, where it rests to this day.”

Composed of one-inch squared blocks, the Trip Around the World Quilt pattern is a variation of a Postage Stamp Quilt.

I mailed a photocopy of the Curtis Roosevelt quilt to Hubert Nukes in hopes that he would recognize the once beloved and well-used covering, now in the permanent collection of a major British museum, as the quilt his grandmother stitched more than seven decades prior.

“I am not sure if this is the same quilt,” Mr. Nukes said during our phone conversation. “It had some yellow in it because of a yellow sweater I got from an uncle.”

In the end, Mr. Nukes could not provide a definitive answer.

According to newspaper reports from 1937, the quilt Estella Nukes and the women of the Marion, Indiana WPA Sewing group made had the initial “F.D.R.” on the quilt. It is unclear if the “F.D.R.” was appliquéd, embroidered, or pieced as part of the quilt’s top or backing.

There is no “F.D.R.” sewn onto Curtis Roosevelt’s Trip Around the World Quilt, confirming, unfortunately, that it is not Hubert Nukes’ grandmother’s covering.

Mrs. Estella Weaver Nukes passed away after a two-week illness on Saturday, August 28, 1937, just months after several African American newspapers from across the country published reports of the Postage Stamp Quilt gift she and others made for President Franklin Roosevelt and mailed to the White House. She was forty-nine years old. The notice of her death said she “had been active in social and civic projects for many years.”

Despite my best efforts, I haven’t been able to uncover what happen to the Postage Stamp Quilt or where it might be today.

Perhaps a distant relative of Mrs. Nukes or one of the women in the Marion WPA Sewing Group has a photograph or more details about the Postage Stamp Quilt or the Thank You note from the White House.

Maybe somewhere in the magical depths of the Library of Congress there is a clue still waiting to be discovered.

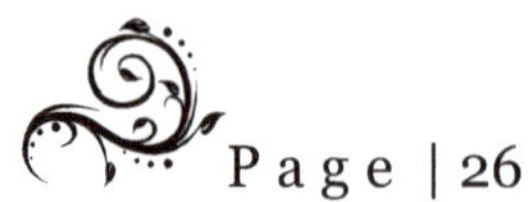

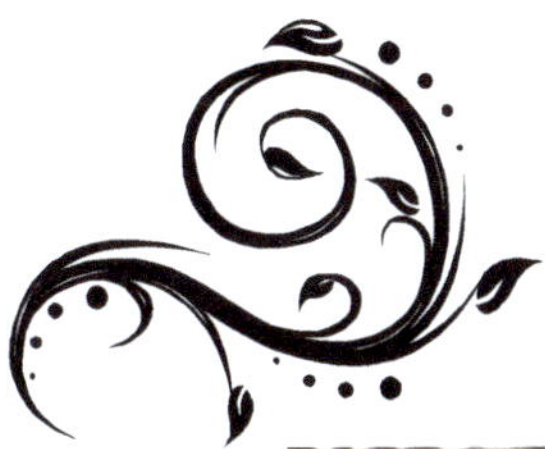

Estella's Family Tree

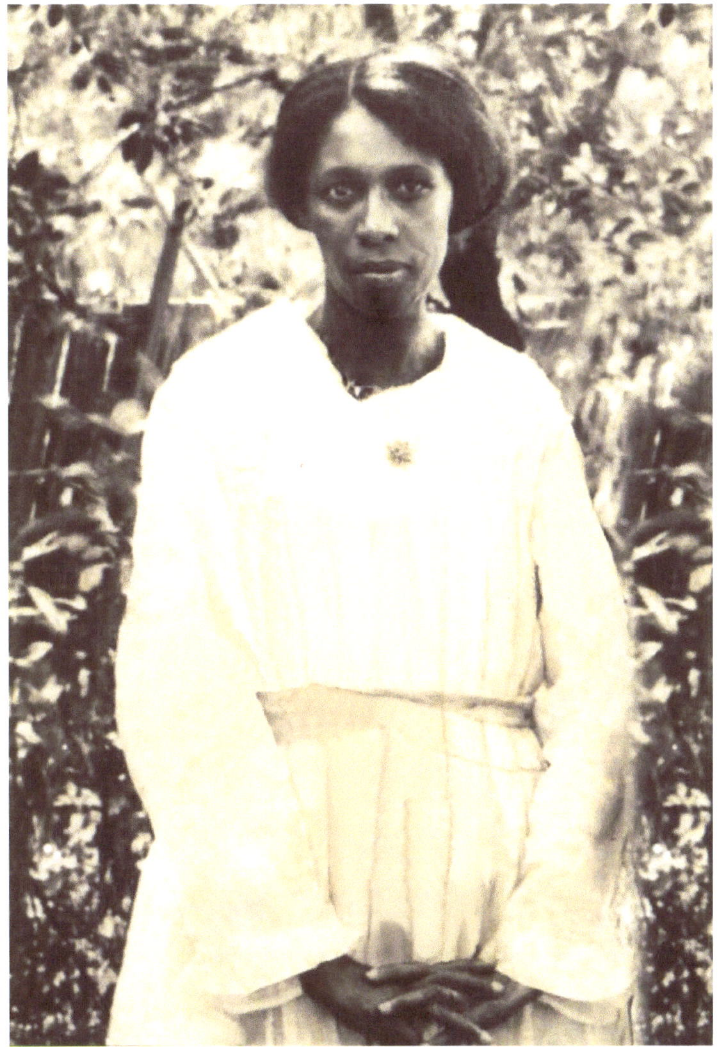

Estella May Weaver Nukes

January 28, 1888 – August 28, 1937
Married June 20, 1906
Home: 1919 South Meridian Street, Marian, Indiana

Parents

Franklin Weaver & Catharine Jones Burden Weaver

Siblings

Archie L. Weaver, Chicago, Illinois

Col. George E. Weaver, Chicago, Illinois

Deborah Dodson, Marion, Indiana

Dr. William H. Burton, Benton Harbor, Michigan

Elwood Weaver, Logansport, Indiana

Thomas Weaver, Marion, Indiana

Myrtle B. Story, Atlantic City, New Jersey

Emma Frazier, Marion, Indiana

Husband

Thomas J. Nukes
January 8, 1873 - May 2, 1941

Children

Ruth Louise Nukes – b. 1906

Walter Archie Nukes – b. 1908

Catherine Rebecca Nukes Folden – b. 1909

Thomas W. Nukes – b. about 1910

Taylor Pierce/Pierson Nukes – b. 1913

Elizabeth Jane Nukes Bowlds – b. 1915

George E. Nukes– b. 1917

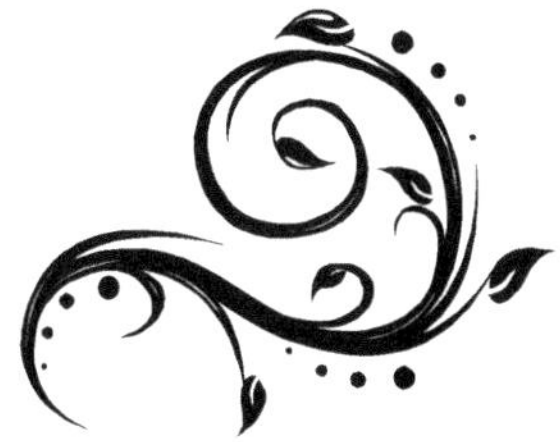

White House Quilt Block

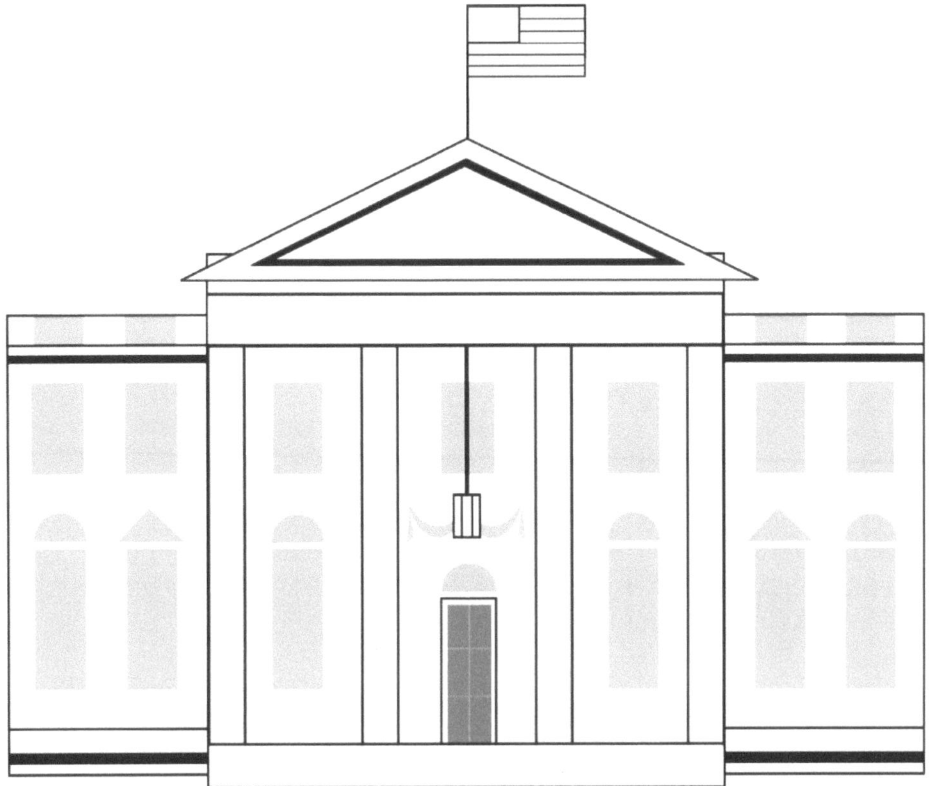

In honor of Estella Weaver Nukes, here is a simplified White House drawing you can use for an appliquéd or redwork quilt block. You can repeat the outer two panels so that your White House has the correct number of windows on each floor.

A special thanks to Mary Ellen Carrier, who took my sketch and created this more polished Presidential home.

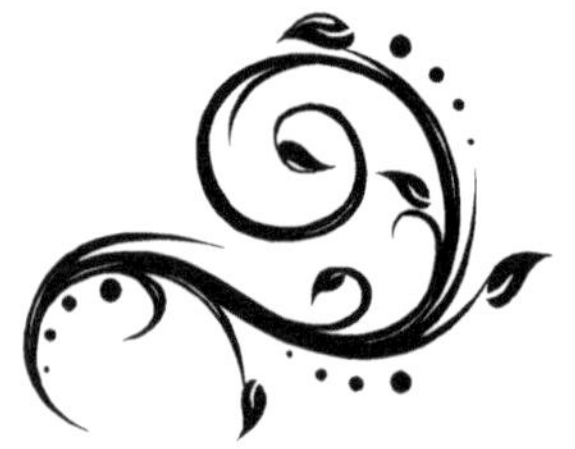

References & Resources

References corresponding to the essay:

Baur, Brian C. Franklin D. Roosevelt: The Stamp-Collecting President. Sidney, OH: Linn's Stamp News, 1999.

Benberry, Cuesta, and Carol P. Crabb. Love of Quilts: A Treasury of Classic Quilting Stories. Stillwater, MN: Voyageur Press, 2004. The "Timeline" section includes selected Roosevelt presidential and quilt history milestones.

Brackman, Barbara. Encyclopedia of Pieced Quilt Patterns. Paducah, KY: American Quilter's Society, 1993.

Cameron, James. A Time of Terror: A Survivor's Story. Baltimore, MD: Black Classic, 1994.

Cleveland, Catharine. "The WPA Sewing Program," Journal of Home Economics, vol. 33, 1941, pp. 588-589. Catharine Cleveland headed the WPA Sewing program nationally.

"Colored Reports." Marion Chronicle. 20 August 1937, p. 2. Notice of Estella Nukes passing. An untitled notice also appeared in the Chronicle-Tribune (Marion, IN), 29 August 1937, p. 16.

"Death of Catherine Weaver: Woman That Caused Rev. Carter's Down Fall Passes Away." Marion Chronicle, 22 July 1897.

"Designs Quilt, Gives It to Pres. Roosevelt." Philadelphia Tribune, 31 December 1936, p. 3.

Frauenberger, Michelle. "Re: Stamp Quilt." Email to Kyra Hicks, 15 June 2007. List of quilts in the Franklin D. Roosevelt Presidential Library and Museum permanent collection.

Ganz, Cheryl R. and Daniel A. Piazza with M.T. Sheahan. Delivering Hope: FDR & Stamps of the Great Depression. Washington DC: Smithsonian National Postal Museum, 2009.

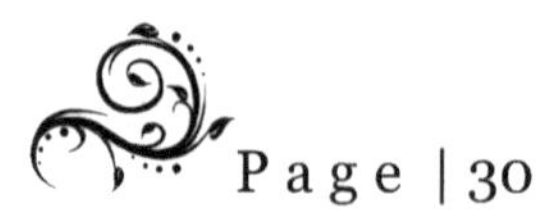

Glenn, R.L. to President and Mrs. Roosevelt, 20 March 1936. Letter regarding quilt by the Negro Home-making Class. Collection of the Franklin D. Roosevelt Library, FDR Gift File.

LeHand, M. A. to R.L. Glenn, 28 March 1936. Letter thanking the Negro Home-making Class for quilt. Collection of the Franklin D. Roosevelt Library, FDR Gift File.

Madison, James H. A Lynching in the Heartland: Race and Memory in America. New York: Palgrave, 2001.

Marcketti, Sara B. "The Sewing-Room Projects of the Works Progress Administration," Textile History, vol. 41, May 2010, pp. 28-49.

Miller, Jerry. "People of Color: Grant County's Black Heritage." Chronicle-Tribune Magazine (Marion, IN), 9 July 1978, pp. 4 – 13.

Moody, Ken. "Re: Quilts." Email to Kyra Hicks, 27, March 2010. Relays Curtis Roosevelts' comments about his own Postage Stamp Quilt.

"Mrs. M'Millan Dies Suddenly: Heart Attack is Fatal to Widely Known Local Woman, Rites Pending." Marion Leader-Tribune, 30 April 1949, pp. 1, 2.

Musso, Anthony. FDR and the Post Office: A Young Boy's Fascination, a World Leader's Passion. Bloomington, IN: Author House, 2006.

Musso, Anthony. "Re: FDR and Postage Stamp Quilt." Email to Kyra Hicks. 29 June 2012.

Nukes, Herbert H. Telephone interviews with Kyra E. Hicks, 8 December 2009, 20 March 2010 and 20 April 2010.

Nukes, Herbert H. Typed family remembrances composed after 1997: "Home," "My Blessings," two different "Reflections," and "Your Grandfather and His Family." Courtesy of Lynn Rude.

"Noted Case Recalled: Mysterious Circumstances Attending Mrs. Weaver's Death." Marion Chronicle, 23 July 1897.

"Novel Quilt is Given to President." New Journal and Guide (Norfolk, VA), 16 January 1937, p. 20.

Parks, Lillian Rogers to Raleigh DeGeer Amyx, 12 April 1983. Letter regarding Eleanor Roosevelt "Yo-Yo" quilt gift. Collection of Raleigh DeGeer Amyx.

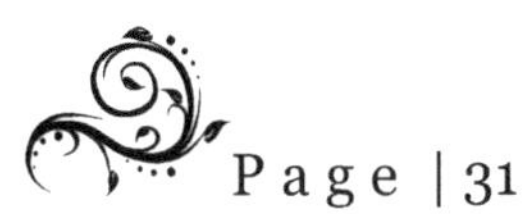

Parks, Lillian Rogers to Raleigh DeGeer Amyx, 20 April 1983. Letter regarding Franklin Roosevelt eagle-themed crochet bedspread gift. Collection of Raleigh DeGeer Amyx.

Parks, Lillian Rogers and Frances S. Leighton. The Roosevelts: A Family in Turmoil. Englewood Cliffs, NJ: Prentice-Hall, 1981.

Patterson, Bradley H. To Serve the President: Continuity and Innovation in the White House Staff. Washington, DC: Brookings Institution Press, 2008. The Correspondence Office, including the Gift Unit, is described on pages 285 – 293.

"President Roosevelt Gets Present of Novel Quilt Designed by Indiana Woman." Pittsburgh Courier, 9 January 1937, p. 3.

"Roosevelt Receives Novel 'Stamp' Quilt." New York Amsterdam News, 2 January 1937, p. 2.

Schilling, Don. "The Ivory Stamp Club." The Stamp Collecting Round-Up. 31 March 2008. Quite interesting and entertaining stamp collecting blog. Visit stampcollectingroundup.blogspot.com

Shawen, Lena Belle. A President's Hobby: The Story of F.D.R.'s Stamps. New York: H. L. Lindquist Publications, 1949.

"Stamp Quilt Is Given to Mr., Mrs. Roosevelt: Indiana Woman's Gift Draws Attention." Chicago Defender, 2 January 1937, p. 4.

Stevenson, Barbara J. An Oral History of African Americans in Grant County. Charleston, SC: Arcadia Publishing, 2000. The Ten-Si-Foy Club is described by Delores Betts on pages 125-126. Photo of the club just before 1900 is on page 123, in 1920 on page 117, and in 1935 on page 92.

Stewart, Elizabeth. Interview by Torrianna Williams, 15 April 1998. http://wikimarion.org/Elizabeth_Stewart. Accessed July 4, 2012.

Still, Robert. "Doug Storer Cleaned Up With Stamps." The Evening Independent (St. Petersburg, FL), 12 October 1981, p. 1. Article about advertising executive Storer creating concept for the *Ivory Stamp Club of the Air* radio program.

Tulley, Grace. F.D.R, My Boss. New York: C. Scribner's Sons, 1949. The book includes several Presidential gift references.

Turner, Patricia A. "I Couldn't *Not* Quilt Obama." American Studies Association, Washington, D.C., November 8, 2009. Dr. Turner presents a four-part classification schema for evaluating Obama-themed quilts primarily created during the 2008 U.S. Presidential Election period.

Wildermuth, Susan. Eye of the Needle, a quilt history blog. Visit the blog at http://sew-eyeoftheneedlequilthistory.blogspot.com. Search keyword "Roosevelt" for blog posts about Roosevelt-inspired quilts. Accessed July 4, 2012.

Whitson, Rolland L, John P. Campbell, and Edgar L. Goldthwait, eds. Centennial History of Grant County, Indiana, 1812 to 1912. Chicago, IL: Lewis Publishing Co., 1914. "The Negro in Grant County" by Mrs. Asenath Peters Artis appears on pages 348-357.

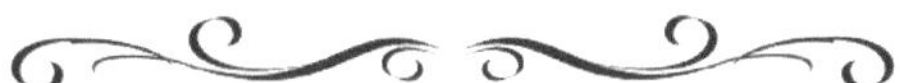

Resources about Presidential Quilts and Quilt Patterns:

American Political Items Collectors, Inc. http://www.apic.us

"The American Presidents Quilt." Aunt Martha's Pattern #7330. Colonial Patterns, Inc., Kansas City, MO. Includes the first through the forty-third presidents.

Bassett, Lynne Zacek. "The Needlework of First Lady Grace Coolidge" PieceWork. Interweave Press, July/August 1999.

Benson, Jane, Nancy Olsen, and Jan Rindfleisch. The Power of Cloth: Political Quilts, 1845-1986. Cupertino, CA: Board of Trustees of the Foothill-De Anza Community College District, De Anza College, 1987. 61 pages.

Borchardt, Terri. The First Ladies Quilt. Lake Mills, WI: Hartington Press, 2010. Quilt block pattern for each First Lady from Martha Washington to Michelle Obama. 111 pages.

Buckingham, Michael G. Presidential Redwork: A Stitch in Time. Paducah, KY: American Quilter's Society, 2000. 80 pages.

Burns, Eleanor. Tales of First Ladies and Their Quilt Blocks. San Marcos, CA: Quilt in a Day, 2011.

Christopherson, Katy. The Political and Campaign Quilt. Lexington, Kentucky: Kentucky Heritage Quilt Society, 1984. 64 pages.

Cummings, Patricia L. "Martha Washington's Needlework." The Quilter, January 2005, pp. 74 – 77. In-depth article on three known quilted-pieces stitched by Martha Washington and now owned by the Mount Vernon Ladies' Association: the *Unfinished Bedcover* (1790-1800), *The Penn Treaty Counterpane* (circa 1785), and *The Martha Washington Quilt*. Cummings also describes "quilted tributes" to the first lady, such as the block patterns: *Martha Washington Wreath, Martha Washington Star*, and the *Martha Washington Rose Garden*.

Cummings, Patricia L. "Presidents, Parties, and Politics Celebrated in Quilt Blocks." The Quilter, November 2005, pp. 68 – 71. Review of various themed blocks and quilts including: Democratic Donkey quilt, the *Fifty-Four Forty or Fight* star block, the *Lincoln's Platform* block, Jill Jayne-Read's 1976 *Jimmy Who?* Quilt, Grace Simpson's *Use It All* block commemorating President Carter's inflation policy, and various White House blocks. Photographs in the article were taken by James Cummings.

Cummings, Patricia L. "Quilts and Needlework with a Political Association, Part II." The Quilter, March 2005, pp. 84 – 88.

Flamer, Michelle E., curator. The President's House: Their Untold Stories in Quilts, Exhibit hosted by the National Constitution Center, Philadelphia, PA from July 1 to September 5, 2011.

Hinson, Dolores A. "Presidential Quilts." The Antiques Journal, July 1971, pp. 17 – 19. Hinson writes of her research on quilts made for U.S. Presidents, including George Washington, James Madison, James Polk, Warren Harding, Franklin Roosevelt, Dwight Eisenhower, and Lyndon Johnson. Hinson, who passed away in 2002, wrote that she planned a book on Presidential quilts. It's unknown if such a book was published or her papers archived.

Houck, Carter. "Political Designs." Lady's Circle of Patchwork Quilts, November 1992.

Mazloomi, Carolyn. Foreword by Meg Cox. Journey of Hope: Quilts Inspired by President Barack Obama. Minneapolis, MN: Voyageur Press, 2010. 216 pages.

McHone, Laurel. Prick Their Consciences: The Politicization of Sewing in America from the Revolutionary War to the Second World War. Senior Thesis. University of North Carolina, Asheville. 2007.

Meador, Michael M. "Ella Martin's Quilt Comes Home." Quilter's Newsletter Magazine, July/August 1989, p. 16. Article about a quilt Mrs. Martin made for Franklin Roosevelt and the quilt's amazing journey beyond the Roosevelt family.

Nelms, Joyce. "The President's Quilt." Quilt World, February 1978, pp. 5 – 6. According to Nelms, President Calvin Coolidge was taught to sew and knit by his grandmother. Located at the Coolidge Homestead in Plymouth, Vermont is a quilt top stitched in 1882 using the "Tumbling Blocks" pattern. The quilt blocks are said to be made by ten-year old Coolidge under the "careful eye of his grandmother" and pieced into a never-completed quilt top in 1905 by his wife, Grace Goodhue Coolidge. Article includes photograph of the quilt.

Obenchain, Mabel, editor. White House Quilts (New York, NY: Pattern Service, 1978). 50 pages. Includes twenty quilt patterns, with names such as "White House Steps," "Martha Washington's Star," and "Tad Lincoln's Sailboat."

Powell, G. Julie. The Fabric of Persuasion: Two Hundred Years of Political Quilts : September 9-November 19, 2000, Brandywine River Museum, Chadds Ford, PA. Chadds Ford, PA: Brandywine River Museum, 2000. 40 pages.

Powell, Julie. "Quilted Ballots: Political and Campaign Textiles," in On the Cutting Edge" Textile Collectors, Collections, and Traditions, ed. Jeannette Lasansky. Lewisburg, PA: Oral Traditions Project, 1994, pp. 27-33.

"Presidents." McCall's Needlework & Crafts Bicentennial Quilt Book (magazine), 1975, pp.33, 42 – 43. Appliquéd quilt pattern featuring silhouettes, embroidered names and administration dates for the first thirty-six U.S. Presidents. Rosalyn Boxley created the quilt; Margetta Dobias designed the silhouettes.

Quilt Index, The. Online resource about quilts, quiltmaking and quilters. The index does include examples of postage stamp quilts. Visit quiltindex.org.

Shephard, Arlesa J. "Quilts for McKinley: Women's Involvement in Politics." In Uncoverings 2008, ed. Laurel Horton, pp. 137 – 158, Lincoln, NE: American Quilt Study Group, 2008. Excellent article on textiles as presidential campaign items.

Walen, Susan. President Obama: A Celebration in Art Quilts, San Francisco, CA: Blurb.com, 2009. 120 pages.

Waugh, Carol Ann and Phyllis McAllaster Stewart. The First Ladies of America Quilt Book. Patterns honoring each First Lady from Martha Washington to Michelle Obama. Denver, CO: Xcellent Marketing Press, 2010. Available from FirstLadiesQuilt.com.

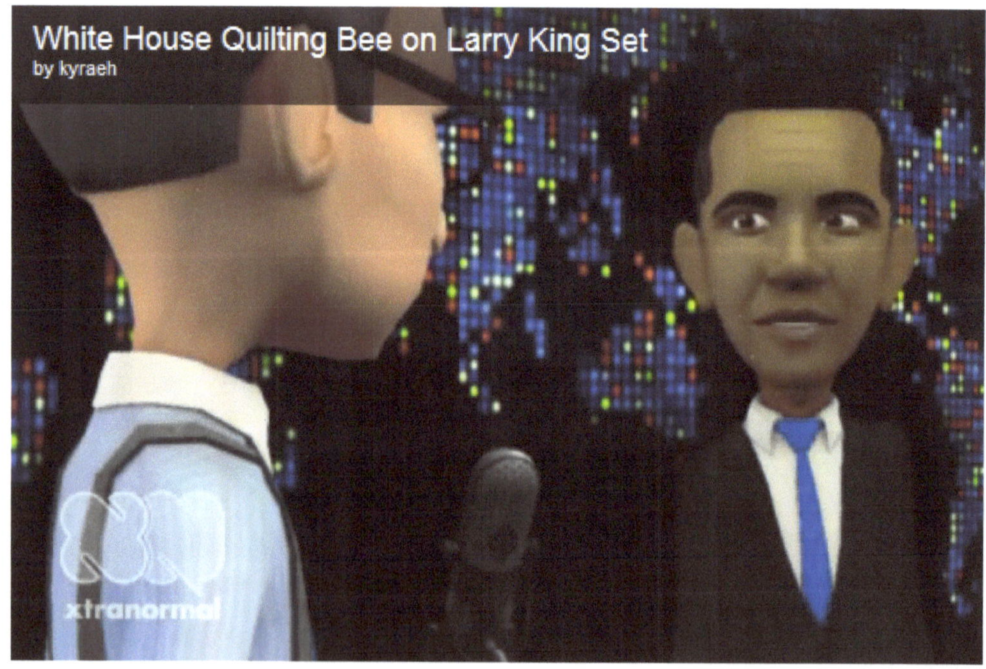

Visit YouTube for this humorous "White House Quilting Bee" video. President Obama is interviewed by talk show host Larry King about a bi-partisan quilting bee he plans to host as a way to explore "common ground" in Washington, DC. 10 December 2010.

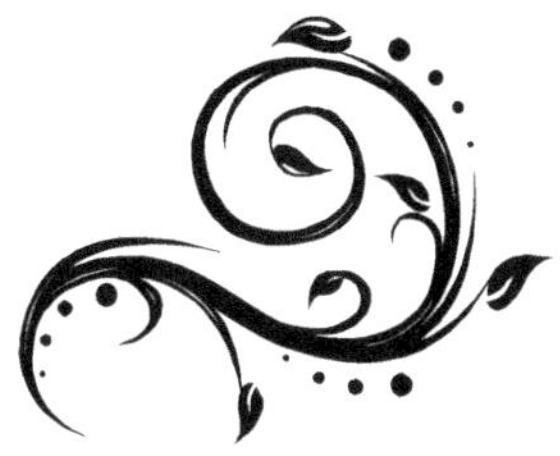

About the Author

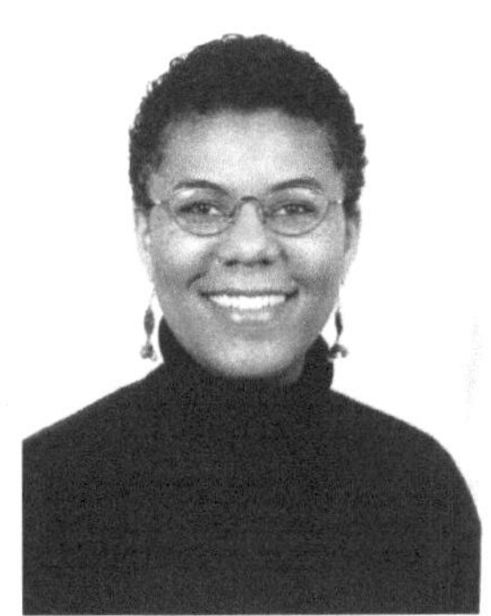

Kyra E. Hicks is a quilter. Her quilts have appeared in more than forty exhibits in the United States and abroad. She loves historical, investigative research and rediscovering the lives of quilters past. Kyra lives in Arlington, Virginia, where she tends her colorful, fragrant rose garden. Visit her at www.BlackThreads.com. Or feel free to write her at Black.Threads@yahoo.com.

You may enjoy Kyra's other books and ebooks:

- *This I Accomplish: Harriet Powers' Bible Quilt and Other Pieces*
- *The Lord's Supper Pattern Book: Imagining Harriet Powers' Lost Bible Story Quilt*
- *How to Self-Publish Your Own Quilt Catalog: A Workbook for Quilters, Guilds, Galleries and Textile Artists*
- *1.6 Million African American Quilters: Survey, Sites, and a Half-Dozen Art Quilt Blocks*
- *Black Threads: An African American Quilting Sourcebook*
- *Martha Ann's Quilt for Queen Victoria*

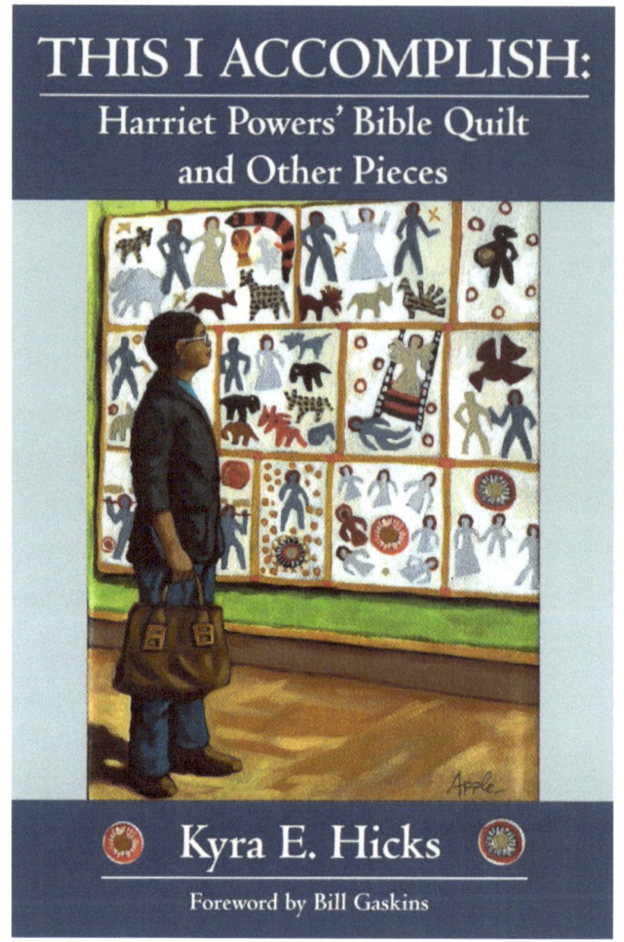

This I Accomplish:
Harriet Powers' Bible Quilt and Other Pieces

The powerful quilts of Harriet Powers (1837-1910), a former Georgia slave, continue to capture our imagination today. Thousands of visitors to the Smithsonian National Museum of American History and the Museum of Fine Arts, Boston have stood transfixed viewing her *Bible Quilt* and *Pictorial Quilt*.

Until now, no one has told the entire, dramatic story of how these quilts (one sold for $5) were cherished in private homes before emerging as priceless national treasures.

"Wow! I kept leaping out of my chair!" said one reader.

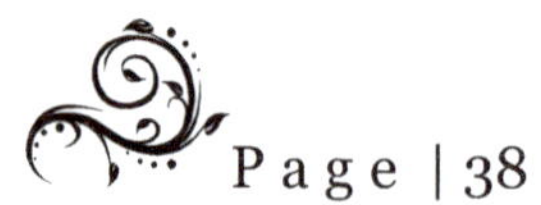

www.ingramcontent.com/pod-product-compliance
Lightning Source LLC
LaVergne TN
LVHW070155110826
845147LV00002B/408

* 9 7 8 0 9 8 2 4 7 9 6 1 2 *